BENEATH JUDICIAL ROBES

An Original Screenplay

based on a true story

by

Don Alexander
31057 Oak Ridge Drive
Rocky Mount, MO
(573) 557-2114

donalexander557@gmail.com

1

CAST OF CHARACTERS

Simon and Dixon LLP	large, extremely wealthy, well connected law firm
Don Alexander	law student at University of Missouri Law School
Danny Alexander	Don's son
Lee Alexander	Don's daughter
Jim Levine	law school professor
Annette Lorry	law school professor
Roy Henz	law school dean
Harry Schmidt	fellow law student
Roland Sanford	president, Missouri State Board of Law Examiners
Harry Meeks	Boone County Prosecuting Attorney
Paula Vaughn	Missouri Bar Committee member

Norman Pratt	Missouri Bar Committee member
Rachael Phelps	Missouri Bar Committee member
Walter Newburg	surrogate, Missouri State Board of Law Examiners
Dale Conley	surrogate's legal counsel
Henry Magene	senior partner, Simon and Dixon Law Firm
Mary Totten	senior appeals partner, Simon and Dixon Law Firm
Herman Dixon	senior partner/owner, Simon and Dixon Law Firm
Sally Watson	staff attorney, Simon and Dixon
Sam Biden	U.S. Attorney, Western District of Missouri
Susan Wright	Assistant Boone County Prosecutor
Bret Heinze	Boone County Public Defender

Judy Schepler	judge, Boone County Circuit Court
Ken Roman	judge, St. Louis County Circuit Court
Adolph Addison	judge, St. Louis County Circuit Court
Henry Grissom	judge, City of St. Louis Circuit Court
Orville White	judge, U.S. District Court, Western District of Missouri
Frank Pippen	judge, U.S. Court of Appeals for the Eighth Circuit
Howard Baker	judge, U.S. Court of Appeals For the Eighth Circuit
Mick Rosen	president, AMI Management Association
Phil	waiter, Clayton, MO restaurant
John	waiter, restaurant in downtown St. Louis

4

FADE IN

INTRODUCTORY LETTERING

This is the true story of Don Alexander's
imprisonment resulting from a criminal
conspiracy involving three law professors, fifteen
lawyers and seven sitting judges.....all of which
should have spent ten years in a federal prison.
The names of professors, lawyers, judges and
various other characters have been changed to
protect innocent parties. Where the script
indicates that Don Alexander was not present,
script continuity is predicated upon what he
actually saw and heard which clearly reveals the
intent of each character.

INT. LARGE MEETING ROOM – NOON

Don stands at podium before sixty or so senior business executives. Don is finishing up a seminar and the attendees are paying close attention. Don taps on headstones engraved Rest In Peace in graveyard identified as Corporate Cemetery illustrated by an overhead projector.

Don

During the past five years, tough and timely decision making by the Chief Executive Officers, assisted by my staff, have kept over 200 corporations out of the corporate cemetery. We have worked with the unions to increase productivity by an average of thirty percent while reducing scrap and rework by more than fifty percent. Our success record is better than 95% because we do not contract with timid or inept chief executives. We are the catalyst that glues all the pieces together. Increased productivity and cost reduction are seldom achieved by the peer level reporting to the chief executive. These senior managers compete with each other for advancement in pay and rank. We do the dirty work with the full approval of the chief executive who contracts with us. If you have the guts to make the tough decisions, we will supply the manpower to ensure timely and successful profit enhancement. Thank you for your attention. Lunch is being served next door.

Several attendees get up and step quickly to podium to confer with Don.

INT. POSH RESTAURANT – DAY

Don sits at elegant table reading newspaper and sipping coffee. Mick Rosen approaches table.

Mick

Good Morning.....

Don looks up and lays aside paper.

Don

Hi....Mick, looks like a great day.

Mick sits down. Waiter in elegant white jacket comes to table.

Waiter

Ahhhhh, my favorite people.....the usual?

Mick

Works for me, Phil......

Don nods okay. Waiter pours coffee for Mick and retreats to fill order.

Don

We just doubled our budgeted income with four months left.

Mick

That's astonishing....but the Board thinks your incentive pay is getting out of hand....and it's causing problems with the other General Managers as well.

Don studies Mick with amused expression.

Don

Let me guess....the Board wants to breach the verbal agreement between you and me.....and steal the incentives that I have earned but can't

collect until the sold projects are actually
completed and all billings paid in full.

Mick

That about sums it up.....why didn't a
bright guy like you insist on a written
employment contract?

Don

For sure.....nothing to it. I just waltz in off
the street and negotiate salary and incentives for
a non-existent operation that no Board member
thinks has a chance of success. Demanding a
written contract covering salary, incentives and
perks pertaining to nothing more than an
operational theory does not make a good
impression..... What about you, Mick.....are you
in on this?

Mick

My contract is coming up for renewal. I don't think it's a good time for me to champion something that the Board does not.

Don

When I agreed to start up and operate a management consulting service within the Association five years ago, I took a peanut salary and relied on incentives to compensate me fairly. Today, the net profit from my operation is greater than the total gross income of the Association when I came on board.

Mick

Now that your operation employs thirteen veteran consultants, the Board figures we can replace you with a polished salesman for less than a hundred grand a year.

Don

Well, Mick. Since your word doesn't count for much, tell the Board I want my earned incentives as the billings are fully paid.....or I'll see you in court.....and I will subpoena you along with AMI's accounting statements covering the last six years.

Mick

I already told them how you would react.

The waiter comes back and begins setting food servings on table. Don drops twenty dollars on table, pushes back his chair and gets up from table.

Don

Good luck, Mick......I hope you can live with this.

Don walks briskly away from table.

INT. DANNY'S APARTMENT – NIGHT

Don and Danny are playing chess on kitchen table.

Both Don and Danny are studying chess board.

Danny makes a move that results in checkmate.

Danny

Dad.....that's three in a row. Where is your mind?

Don looks at Danny with a deep sigh.

Don

I don't know, Son, it's obviously not on chess......and......if it was, you'd probably win

anyway. How are you making out doing your
med school clinical routines?

Danny leans back in chair and laces fingers behind
his head.

Danny

Straight A's.....chip off the old block.
What are you going to do now that AMI has
picked your pockets?

Don

I've been giving that some serious thought.
I think I'll move to Columbia to spend some
quality time with you......and get me a law degree.

Danny

What are you going to do about the five
and a half million AMI confiscated?

Don

I'll file a breach of contract suit if they leave me no other option. I'd like to avoid an extended legal battle.....but my assets are pretty much tied up in the unpaid incentive earnings.....and my credit standing is rapidly disappearing.

SUPER: 2 YEARS LATER.

INT. COURTROOM – DAY

A couple dozen lawyers are either sitting or lounging in courtroom. Sally Watson and Don stand before judge. A bronze name tag on right corner of bench reads "Honorable Ken Roman." Judge has open file in front of him.

Judge Roman

Mr. Alexander, we are here on your motion to compel discovery from the defendant, AMI Management Association, which is appearing through its attorneys, Simon & Dixon. You have filed interrogatories, requests for admissions and for production of documents relative to this case. Have you received any response from AMI?

As judge is addressing Don, Sally is shuffling through her file folder.

Don

No, Your Honor......I have received nothing whatsoever.

Sally looks a little flustered and keeps flipping through her file as if some important document is apparently missing.

Judge Roman

Do you wish to be heard, Ms. Watson?

Sally pulls several pages from her folder and
waves them at judge.

Sally

These are our objections to Mr.
Alexander's discovery requests, Your
Honor....Mr. Alexander has not filed a
certificate of attempt to resolve our
objections.....and therefore his motion to compel
discovery is premature under local discovery
rules.

Judge Roman

I could care less what you have in your
briefcase, Ms. Watson. I am looking at the

official court file and I do not see any notice that AMI or its attorneys have filed any response of any kind to Mr. Alexander's discovery requests. If Mr. Alexander will concur, I will grant you exactly seven days from today to file answers to every discovery item.....and the time for objections expired fifteen days ago.

Judge looks from Sally back to Don while Sally maintains a shocked expression.

Judge Roman

What say you, Mr. Alexander?

Don

The extension of time is agreeable to me.

Judge Roman

So be it! Next case......

EXT. MISSOURI UNIVERSITY LAW
SCHOOL CAMPUS – DAY
Students are strolling about the campus.

CAMPUS CAFETERIA

Harry Schmidt and Don are chatting while eating
breakfast.

Harry

How did you fare with Judge Roman?

Don

*He threatened to default the association and
nearly gave Simon and Dixon's staff attorney a
cardiac seizure.*

Harry

Good for him! Maybe there's still some hope for
the system.
How much time did he give them?

Don

Seven days. That's fairly generous
considering Simon and Dixon were already into
procedural default. But, I did not object. What
irritates me is that I had to drive from Columbia
to St. Louis County for a procedural hearing
lasting three minutes.

Harry

I interviewed with Herman Dixon
Saturday morning. The conversation was more
about you than recruiting me.

Don

How so.......?

Harry

*Herman wanted to know if you are
popular around campus.....being fifty plus.....and
if you 're in the top ten percent. I told him you
already know more law than most judges and
tutor me on the side.*

Don

Kinda stretching the truth a little, I'd say.

Harry

I didn't like the guy.....too pushy.

Don

Better get used to that if you wanna join the club.

INT. SIMON & DIXON'S PLUSH
EXECUTIVE OFFICE --- DAY

Sally Watson approaches door to Henry Magene's private office identified by brass name tag. Sally knocks reverently on fancy wood door, and then waits until Henry opens door. He flashes a friendly smile.

Henry

Afternoon, Sally, come on in.

Henry walks back to executive desk chair and Sally seats herself on visitor's black leather couch. Henry picks up cigar from desk ashtray:

Henry

I understand Judge Roman gave us seven days to answer all discovery requests directed to

AMI from Alexander. Where are we
in this case?

Sally

We can't answer his request for
admissions without getting tossed on summary
judgment, and we have no legal basis for a
protective order. He lucked out and drew Judge
Roman for the hearing on his motion to compel.
We'll have to file incomplete answers and hope
for one of our judges when he refiles to compel.

Henry

We've got five days left on Roman's order
plus the time required to notice us up for another
hearing. I'll pull a few strings and get Judge
Addison assigned to hear our motion for a
protective order. In the meantime, you need to
get our affidavit and motion in the court file to
protect Judge Addison.

Sally

I could be disbarred......the affidavit would be false and I'd have to backdate the motion.

Henry

Just get it done, I'll personally take care of any complaints to the bar.

INT. COURTROOM – DAY

Attorneys are seated in front rows waiting to be heard. Don and Sally are on opposite sides of aisle. The bailiff steps to side of bench and calls next case. The brass name tag on left front corner of bench reads Honorable Adolph Addison.

Bailiff

Alexander versus AMI Management Association......

Don and Sally get up simultaneously and walk briskly to front of bench. The Judge looks at file contents.

Judge

I'm listening.........

Sally

Good Morning, Your Honor. We're here on AMI Management Association's motion for a protective order from unrelated and burdensome discovery requests by Plaintiff per our affidavit supporting our motion. For the reasons stated in our affidavit, Plaintiff has argued nothing nor filed anything to date to justify snooping into AMI's corporate and accounting records.

Sally snaps her file shut as if there is no need to say more. Don looks at her with disgust as judge makes note and looks st Don.

Don

First Your Honor, the discovery requests have already been argued before Judge Roman and he gave AMI seven days to fully comply with every request I submitted. AMI is now in default per that order by five days. Second, AMI seeks to hide the records which will prove my allegations which means that the discovery requests are critical to exposing the truth in this case. Third, AMI's time to object under the Missouri Rules of Civil procedure expired fifteen days before Judge Roman ruled against them. Ms. Watson knowingly filed a false affidavit and backdated her motion for a protective order. She should be disbarred and charged with perjury.

Judge Addison looks down with a blank
expression at the court file open before him.

Judge Addison
*AMI Management Association's motion
for a protective order is granted.*

Don's jaw drops open in amazement.

INT. LAW SCHOOL CLASSROOM --- DAY

Ethics lecture is in progress. Professor Levine
stands at podium before fifty or so law students.

Levine
*That is why we have a reporting obligation.
Your's is a self-policing profession that is
wholly responsible for the integrity of the*

legal system. That is why you will all be officers of the court. The Missouri Supreme Court has adopted and published a protocol for reporting any ethics violation. The Missouri Bar is vested to hear complaints and take appropriate action up to and including temporary or permanent disbarment.

Harry is seated in middle of class next to Don; Harry has hand raised.

Levine

Question.....Mr. Schmidt?

Harry

What happens when obvious ethics violations are just ignored or continue, for whatever reason, to remain unreported?

Levine

Then, ladies and gentlemen.....Blind Justice becomes a diseased whore and the public rightly loses all respect for law and order.

EXT. MISSOURI UNIVERSITY CAMPUS CAFETERIA --- DAY

Don and Harry are seated at table eating burger and fries with coffee. Harry pauses, swallows and looks toward ceiling.

Harry

I don't believe lawyers routinely rat on one another. If you wanna play with the "big guys," you gotta protect the brotherhood.

Don puts down burger and sips his coffee. He looks toward center of table and nods agreement.

Don:

I was a cop back in my twenties and I still think about the rampant corruption I saw in the courts and among prosecutors and public defenders who advanced their careers at the expense of the poor and underprivileged.....and lawyers with the least morals were appointed to the bench. Why you wanna be a mouthpeice, Harry?

Harry lays down burger, wipes mouth and looks thoughtfully at Don.

Harry:

I'm looking for something more mentally challenging than selling real estate. I kinda like the idea of butting heads with self-perceived intellectuals. How about you? You're certainly not here for the money.

Don chews a bite of burger and reflects on Harry's question. He sips some coffee and grins at Harry.

Don:

I've been to the top of the mountain.....and didn't like the company. I'd like to dedicate the rest of my productive life to helping those who can't afford competent legal counsel. A modest apartment and a cheap car serves the same purpose as a mansion and Rolls Royce. The question is.....what do you want to take with you to the grave? You can't take money nor possessions.....so why bother sacrificing principles for vanity?

Harry

That's pretty heavy....but I feel the same way. I have no desire to flaunt wealth and status by stomping on others. That's why I like being around you. We think alike....so, how do we beat up on the bad guys?

Don

Let's hope we don't have to adopt the Rawlings' method.

Harry

Never heard of it. What's the Rawlings'method?

Don wipes mouth and shoves plate back.

Don

I did a consulting job in Ghana, Africa roughly eight years ago. The total

corruption of law and order was transparent.
Right after I left Africa, an army Lieutenant
named Rawlings led the masses in revolt. They
loaded up the corrupt politicians, lawyers and
judges into cattle trucks, hauled them out into a
field and shot them dead. Rawlings and his
followers closed the borders until a new
government was elected and assumed control of
t he country.

Harry

Wow!....that's a pretty effective method.
Kinda like the French Revolution
when the peasants finally had enough of the
feudal system.

Don

Millions of individuals have willingly
sacrificed themselves to fight against the

corruption of law and order. I'd like to think there is a more bloodless way to defend our constitutional rights......like exposing the brotherhood.

Harry

Suits me.....I prefer the pen over the sword.

INT. COURTROOM – DAY

Court is in session. Judge Addison is addressing Don and Sally.

Judge Addison

I concur with Ms. Watson, Mr. Alexander, that no evidence has been offered to show bias in this case. I am inclined to deny your motion for a change of venue.

34

Don

Your Honor, AMI did not file any hardship objections nor any other objections opposing the venue change. Under the Missouri rules, I am entitled to change of venue as of right. You have no authority to deny me what the rules grant as of right.

Judge's facial expression is noticeably hostile and Sally looks down at floor in surprise.

Judge Addison

Bailiff.....bring me the Missouri rules.

Bailiff opens door from courtroom to judge's chamber, disappears and immediately reappears with rules book in hand. He walks to bench and hands book to judge. Judge Addison silently reads the motion for change of venue rules. There is dead silence in courtroom. Judge's hand trembles slightly and his voice betrays his anger.

Judge Addison

*I'll grant you a change of venue Mr.
Alexander......from the county circuit to the city
circuit. Goodbye, Mr. Alexander.*

Don

*Your Honor, my motion clearly alleges
that Simon and Dixon exerts undue influence in
both St. Louis County and the City of St. Louis.*

Judge Addison

The matter is settled. My ruling is final.

Don

*You leave me no choice, your Honor. I
will file a writ of mandamus, a complaint to the
Commission on Discipline and Retirement of
Judges; and appeal the matter all the way to the
United States Supreme Court based on denial of
due process and equal protection of the laws.*

The courtroom remains totally quiet and fixated. Judge Addison gets up from bench and stalks through door into his chambers.

INT. PIZZA PARLOR – DAY

Don and Danny are sitting at table eating pizza and drinking soda. Don chases slice of pizza with soda and gazes at Danny.

                    Don

          Your mother helping you any with
                tuition and books?

                   Danny

      Not really. She and Terry just built a
    house and are strapped for cash, so I don't
    expect anything. I'm getting by with school loans
       and working part-time with computers.

Don

I'm getting stonewalled in court. I doubt that I'll see any breach of contract money before you graduate. That really upsets me. Lee needs a car to travel between her classes and clinical locations. She's now over at Deaconess Hospital and commuting to Faith West Medical Center.

Danny

*Don't sweat it Dad.....we can both take care of ourselves.
Go ahead and make those turkeys pay up.*

INT. PROFESSOR LEVINE'S CLASSROOM – DAY

Constitutional law lecture is in progress.

Levine

Violation of civil rights confers standing to file suit in federal court. The complaint may allege deprivation of any rights guaranteed under the United States Constitution.....such as due process, equal protection, right to confront witnesses; right to jury trial; and right to counsel. Civil rights violation is a federal felony and damages inflicted by such violation are recoverable in federal court. Civil rights violation reported to federal prosecutors are investigated by the FBI. Conviction means up to ten years in a federal prison.

Levine looks at his watch and begins gathering his notes. Don and Harry close books, get up and exit classroom together. Harry chuckles softly.

Harry

Hear that my friend....you got equal protection of the laws......tell it to the judge; tell him Professor Levine said so.

Don

That ought to scare Addison right out of his chambers.

INT. SIMON & DIXON'S EXECUTIVE OFFICE --- DAY Henry Magene sits at his desk reading legal document. Herman Dixon opens door to Henry's office and sticks head in. He looks worried.

Herman

Got a minute, Henry?

Henry

Come in, Herman....and have a seat. Whatcha need?

Herman enters, seats himself and squints at Henry with obvious concern.

Herman

AMI is getting extremely nervous and wants a senior partner assigned to the case. This pro se law student is making our judges more than a little nervous. We need to step on him a bit harder.

Henry

Its in the works. Judge Addison will send Alexander to the equity division where Judge Grissom will side with us and give him the boot.

Herman

Alexander cannot be allowed to sit for the bar exam...he is bad news.

Henry

Mary is going to make sure he gets a brutal oral exam by the Bar Committee, and gets denied permission by the Law Board to sit for the exam.

Henry pushes button on phone to speak with secretary.

Henry

Marge, ask Mary Totten to join us.

Herman

*You better cover our tracks very carefully.
If this troublemaker ever gets past the bar exam,
he's going to be a constant thorn in our side.*

Mary Totten opens door, enters office and sits
down across from Henry.

Mary

*Hi....guys. What's going on.....I'm
due in court shortly.*

Henry

*Briefly bring Herman up to date on
our plans for Alexander.*

Mary

*We've hired a private detective to dig up
something in his past to conflict with his*

statements in his application to sit for the bar exam. The Bar Committee is going to cooperate with us and I have discussed the matter with the other four members on the Law Board. We are going to deny his application. He won't practice law in Missouri.

Herman

Don't get careless and let this problem get too big for us to manage at the state level. I'd hate to collect my IOU's from the Eighth Circuit bench.

INT. BOWLING ALLEY – NIGHT

Don and Lee are enjoying some father and daughter bonding. Don stands at alley delivery line with bowling ball poised, sighting down alley. Lee munches on big cheeseburger. Don delivers ball and leaves a ten pin. Lee watches and chews burger while Don throws a spare. Don returns to seat behind scorecard buttons. Lee lays aside burger and sips her soda.

Lee

I needed that....I haven't eaten since breakfast.

Don

*Take your time, Sweetheart....we're
in no hurry.
Go ahead and finish eating.*

Lee continues consuming her burger. Don sits
beside her.

Lee

*Danny tells me that you're worried
about me needing a car.*

Don

*I'd buy you a new one if I could.....I'll try
to find something for you to get by with until I
get my money from AMI.*

Lee finishes her burger and wipes her mouth with
napkin.

Lee

I'm okay, Dad. I got a ride for now and I have a part-time job lined up. I'll find me something I can afford. Please don't fret about me.

Don

I know you can take care of yourself. It just makes me want to strangle those thieves at AMI. I'll make it up to you......one way or another.

INT. COURTROOM – DAY

Don and Henry Megene are standing at bench before judge. The bench name tag identifies judge as Honorable Henry Grissom. Megene is addressing the bench in a lofty tone.

Magene

*Your Honor, we have resubmitted our
motion for a protective order
alleging that the discovery requested is not
relevant; and that the facts pled
indicate a claim in equity rather than civil
damages.*

Don

*Your Honor, I have a writ of mandamus
pending plus two formal complaints alleging
ethics violations and perjury on the part of
AMI's attorneys. Judge Roman ordered AMI to
forthwith answer my discovery requests. Those
long overdue answers are directly related to
proving an oral contract falling within the
parole evidence rule and showing that AMI
currently is stealing five and a half million
dollars from me.*

Judge Grissom stares at open file atop the bench.

Judge Grissom

*The appellate court will decide the
mandamus issue. I concur that this is a case in*

equity which is hereby transferred to the equity division for a bench trial. The defendant's protective order is granted..

INT. LAW SCHOOL LIBRARY – DAY

Don is sitting at library research table taking case notes. There are a dozen law books cluttering the table. Harry approaches table with friendly grin.

Harry

Hi, Don. What's been happening in the big city?

Don looks up, lays pen aside, and smiles at Harry. Harry sits down at table.

Don

Simon and Dixon have apparently spread some very serious money around both the county and city circuits. They own most of the judges and can pull enough strings to get me in front of their most ardent puppet. I'm wasting my time in

47

state court. I'll have to file a complaint in
federal court alleging a conspiracy to violate my
civil rights.......due process and equal protection
of the laws.

Harry

It's about time for the peasants to come
screaming out of the fields.....or maybe to
dethrone some political scalawags hidden
beneath judicial robes. What's next? You'll have
to file the federal complaint in the district
court in Kansas City.

Don

Orville White is the U.S. District Judge. I
wonder how many political favors he owes for
getting him appointed to the bench.
We shall see......

INT. PROFESSOR'S LEVINE'S OFFICE –
DAY

Levine is sitting at his desk working at his
computer. The door to his office is open. Don
appears in doorway.

Don

Afternoon....Professor. Got time to chat a few minutes?

Levine looks from computer to Don, smiles pleasantly and leans back in swivel chair.

Levine

For you, I'll make time. Come on in....

Don enters office, pulls up chair across from Levine and pulls notes from inside jacket pocket.

Don

I figured you might appreciate being updated on some ethics violations. Simon and Dixon intentionally filed a false affidavit and backdated a motion for a protective order......then managed to schedule a hearing based upon that double perjury before Judge Addison. Addison granted the motion for a protective order and became blind, deaf and dumb when I pointed out the perjury in the court file open in front of him. I then filed for a change of venue. Simon and Dixon filed nothing in response to allegations of facts contained in my motion. Addison first simply denied the venue change, then sent me to the city circuit when I pointed out that he had no authority to deny me a change of venue as of right. Judge Grissom in the city circuit transferred the case to the equity division to cut me off from a jury trial. How does that grab you for a highly ethical, self-policing profession in action involving recognized officers of the court?

Levine appears visibly shaken and rocks forward in his chair.

Levine

*How much of this summary
can you prove?*

Don

All of it.....I obtained a certified copy of the court record before Simon and Dixon or their accomplices could alter or destroy the incriminating evidence.....pretty sloppy of them I'd say.

Levine's expression switches to thoughtfulness.

Levine

What are you planning to do?

Don

*I ought to stab each of them in the ear
with an icepick. Mary Totten, senior appeals
partner at Simon and Dixon, sits on the
Missouri State Board of Law Examiners. I fully
expect the Law Board to deny me permission to
sit for the bar exam. I just finished a very hostile
oral examination by the local bar committee
after a private detective conducted a blanket
investigation of my background from birth to the
present time.*

Levine folds hands in front of himself and stares at
his desktop.

Levine

*That's the most incredible example of
ethics violations and civil rights conspiracy that I
have ever heard. This calls for disbarment of
lawyers involved, removal of judges taking part
in the conspiracy....and up to ten years in prison*

for each conspirator. What are you expecting from me, Don?

Don takes time to carefully consider Levine's question.

Don

Nothing.....just thought you would be interested since you wrote the ethics rules adopted by the Missouri Supreme Court.....and teach both ethics and constitutional law here in the state university. You wanna hear Professor Lorry's response to this criminal behavior by lawyers and judges?

Levine cringes and avoids Don's gaze.

Levine

What did she say?

Don answers in a mocking voice.

Don

Ahhhhh........I just can't get involved.

Levine appears dumbstruck and presses his fingers against his brow. He looks at ceiling and shakes his head sadly.

Levine

Annette wants to be a federal judge as badly as I want a judgeship anywhere. Anyone wanting a judgeship sitting anywhere in Missouri has to maintain total support by the Missouri Bar.

Don

That's why I'm not asking for your help, Jim. I hope both you and Annette get your appointments. Well....I'd best continue researching federal case law.

Don get up and exits the office. Levine laces fingers behind head and closes his eyes to fight back tears.

INT. HENRY MAGENE"S OFFICE – DAY

Henry is on his office phone. Mary Totten opens door and sticks head in. Henry signals her to be

seated. She enters, sits down. Henry winds up
telephone conversation.

Henry

*Okay, Judge, we'll take care of
the problem today.*

Henry hangs up, then pushes button for secretary.

Henry

Marge, hold my calls.

Mary's voice reeks with deep concern.

Mary

*The Bar Committee recommended
Alexander be seated for the bar exam. They're
afraid of an FBI investigation. The Committee
can be a real problem if subpoenaed by
Alexander in a federal hearing alleging a civil
rights conspiracy.*

Henry replies with a cocky tone.

Henry

The U.S. Attorney would have to initiate such an investigation and he will not expend federal funds chasing Alexander's complaints. Both Sam Biden and Judge White will ignore Alexander if we burn some IOU's in the Western District. If Sam doesn't boot the complaints as federal prosecutor, Orville will as U.S. District Judge.

Mary

The Law Board at my insistence has denied Alexander permission to sit for the bar and the denial letter has gone out. You better contact Sam and Orville so they know what's coming.

Henry

*I will....and I'd better update Herman
before I make those calls.*

INT. CLERK'S OFFICE, US COURTHOUSE IN
KANSAS CITY – DAY

Don hands legal filings to clerk who stamps two
copies of each document and hands the duplicate
copies to Don. Don waves thanks and leaves
clerk's office, then walks to courtroom door and
reads name above door, Honorable Orville White.
Don walks on and finds office of U.S. Attorney
for the Western District of Missouri. The name on
door is Sam Biden, U.S. Attorney/Federal
Prosecutor.

Don enters office and lays written complaint upon counter. A clerical comes up and picks up the document.

Don

This is a formal complaint for conspiracy to violate my civil rights pertaining to due process, equal protection of the laws and various other rights as determined by the United States Supreme Court. Tell Mr. Biden that I will call him after he has an opportunity to review my complaint. I live in Columbia, Missouri.....which is in the Western District and I am a third year law student at the UMC campus.

Don signs date and time blocks and walks away.

INT. ROLAND SANDFORD'S OFFICE – DAY

Roland is sitting at desk writing on a legal pad. His phone buzzes. Roland punches button with irritated expression.

Roland

Yes, Maggie......

Voice over intercom

Mary Totten is here to see you.

Roland:

Good.....send her in.

The door opens and Mary enters. Roland smiles a greeting.

Roland

Good to see you Mary. Like some coffee?

Mary sits down across from Roland's desk.

Mary

No thanks. I've had my limit already.

Roland

Did you invite Judge White to our Law Board social?

Mary

Yes....I did. He thought that you as president of the Board should have extended the invitation. Helen told me his feelings were hurt.

Roland

I didn't realize he's so sensitive about status protocol. I'll send him a special invitation by messenger service before lunch.

Mary

I think that will soothe his judicial ego.....We have another situation that needs attention.

59

Someone's helping Alexander draft his complaints. They are too tight and legally proper to be prepared by a mere law student......any idea who is helping him?

Roland

We've already made sure that no practicing lawyer in this state will dare take his case......so that leaves only judges, law professors and perhaps retired members of the bar. The most likely law professors are Jim Levine and Annette Lorry. I doubt that any sitting judge is assisting him. It has to be law professors or retired members of the bar.

Mary

I agree. Why don't you speak with Roy Henz and make sure he gets the message out to every faculty member that no professor is to assist Alexander under any circumstances.

Roland

I'll speak with Henz about it over dinner tonight. We also have to make absolutely sure that Alexander doesn't get access to any state records or other incriminating evidence through discovery procedures during his administrative appeal before the Law Board surrogate. I'll get Judge White to classify his case as frivolous which will cut off discovery and get the case thrown out of court.

Mary's concerned expression changes to a sly grin.

Mary

I spoke with my pet reporter at the Columbia Tribune and mentioned that a rogue law student may contact the paper

seeking publicity.

Roland

Excellent move! Without admissible

evidence the paper will see nothing newsworthy

except a law student denied permission to sit for

the Bar Exam.

Mary

He won't be able to conduct discovery

during his administrative appeal.

I spoke with our surrogate, Walter Newburg, and

his appointed counsel, Dale Conley. They will

cover the files with a blanket of confidentiality

and declare the discovery unrelated to the issues

to be decided by our surrogate.

Roland

Walter and Dale are old friends. They'll

cooperate with us all the way......including

gutting his appeal to the Missouri Supreme Court. I'm sure that Alexander will appeal the turn-down by our surrogate.

Mary gets up and opens the door. Roland stands up as a courtesy.

Mary

That should get him out of our hair.

INT. PROFESSOR LORRY'S OFFICE – DAY

The office door is open. Don knocks softly on door frame and looks in. Professor Lorry looks up from her computer.

Don

Excuse me Professor.....do you have time to answer a couple of quick questions on federal procedures?

Lorry

Depends.....what do you want me

to comment on?

Don enters office and sits down across from Lorry.

Don

Are there any judicial immunity issues not

covered in class that I should be aware

of........and, are there any special evidence rules

that apply to allegations charging a civil rights

conspiracy?

A stunned expression crosses Lorry's face from which she quickly recovers.

Lorry

I'm sorry. I cannot comment on your situation.

Don locks eyes with Lorry.

Don

Are you a licensed attorney, member of the Missouri Bar, and professor of federal procedures at the state university or a two-faced imposter kissing ass in pursuit of a seat on the federal bench?

Lorry studies Don with a wise owl demeanor.

Lorry

You know that I cannot give you legal advice since I am not your attorney.

Don

I am not seeking legal advice. I am a law student asking my federal procedures professor a question relevant to my law school education.

Lorry

You have also filed a civil rights
conspiracy suit and criminal charges against
members of the Missouri Bar.

Don

Professor Lorry, multiple ethics violations
by other Missouri Bar members are happening
right under your nose. I know that you are
aware of the ethics violations as well as the
criminal behavior involved. What about your
sworn oath as an officer of the court to report
any and all ethics violations in order to maintain
a self-policing legal profession?

Lorry

I choose not to get involved. I have a
class to prepare for.
Please shut the door on your way out.

INT. HERMAN DIXON'S OFFICE – DAY

Herman is smoking pipe and reading legal document. He puffs pipe rapidly, looking very concerned. He stops reading and gazes up at ceiling. There is a gentle knock on his door. Henry Magene opens door and is waved in by Herman. Henry enters, seats himself and Herman lays aside his pipe. Henry looks very perturbed.

Henry

__Looks like our problem with Alexander is mushrooming out of control. He has filed criminal charges against us and a damage suit in federal court.__

Herman leans back in his chair, folds hands over his stomach and replies in a declarative tone.

Herman

This guy thinks he can put us in the slammer. I was just reading his complaint that Sam sent me. Judge White is livid. Alexander's suit alleges both conspiracy and perjury and we all know we're guilty as charged. Making this whole thing go away is going to get extremely expensive. Alexander has some very incriminating evidence.

Henry

We should have seen this coming after he filed ethics violations against us. He's gonna take us all the way to the U.S. Supreme Court. If I were in his shoes, that is precisely what I would do.

Herman picks up his pipe and relights it. Henry says nothing.

Herman

You better personally go and conference with Judge White in the privacy of his chambers. Make whatever deal will buy his cooperation. We need to get the suit thrown out as totally frivolous. If Alexander does file a federal appeal, we've got reliable friends on the Circuit bench. I've scheduled drinks and dinner with Justices Pippen and Baker......to discuss a possible appeal.

INT. PROFESSOR LEVINE'S DINING ROOM – EVENING

Levine is dining with his wife and two teenage sons. The telephone in the living room rings. Levine wipes mouth, gets up, walks to living room and picks up phone.

Levine:

Jim Levine.....

Voice on phone

Roy Henz, Jim.....sorry to bother you at home.....but a rather serious matter has been dumped on me that I need to pass along immediately.

Levine

No problem, Roy.....what's up?

Henz

The Law Board, Bar Committee, and several judges believe a faculty member is helping Don Alexander draft his pleadings and prepare for pretrial hearings. Herman Dixon mentioned you and Professor Lorry.

Levine

Don is quite capable of pleading his own case. But....you know the system.....he needs a very competent attorney because of judicial prejudice against pro se plaintiffs.

Henz

That's his problem....not ours. I just had dinner with Roland Sanford. He made it very clear that anyone who helps Alexander will be blackballed throughout the state. I know how badly you and Annette want a judgeship.

Levine

It appears that Don is right about a civil rights conspiracy involving lawyers, judges, and Missouri Supreme Court appointees.

Henz

I don't like it either, Jim. I just thought you should be aware of the threat......right from the horse's mouth.

Levine hangs up phone with a trembling hand.

INT. JUDGE ROMAN'S CHAMBERS – DAY

The actual chambers opens to a work desk and files for the judge's clerk. The clerk is at her desk and the judge's door is open. Don enters clerk's area and greets clerk. Judge looks through door, sees Don and waves him in. Don enters chambers and stands before judge's desk.

Don

Good morning, Your Honor.....thank you for seeing me.

Judge Roman

I hear you're involved in some pretty heavy litigation and filing some criminal charges. Take my advice, Don. Forget the Law Board and Missouri Bar and get on with your life. You'll never get the coon out of that tree.

Don

That's probably the best advice I've heard....sound's like you know all about my situation.

Judge gets up from desk and closes door to chambers, sits down again.

Judge Roman

Yeah.....but, I've seen a lot worse. Are you still representing yourself?

Don

Not by choice.....no lawyer wants my case enough to risk being stomped on by the Missouri Bar. I just stopped by, Judge, to ask if you will testify for me regarding your order to AMI to answer my discovery requests.....which Simon and Dixon ignored.

Judge Roman

I will if you subpoena me. I'm not allowed to volunteer my testimony.

Don

Thank you, Your Honor. I won't issue a subpoena unless it becomes absolutely necessary to prove perjury.

Don turns away to exit. Judge Roman adds a little encouragement.

Judge Roman

I know a good attorney who might take your case. He's a former judge and county prosecutor and will take on the devil......Russ Short......give him a call and tell him I recommended him to you.

Don

Thank you again, Your Honor.....I'll call him right now.

Don exits Judge Roman's chambers and walks down hallway between courtrooms to pay phone booth, looks up number in hanging phone book, and dials Russ Short. Phone rings and Short's secretary answers:

Secretary on phone

Mr. Short's office......

Don

This is Don Alexander......Judge Roman
suggested I ask Mr. Short to represent me......is
he in?

Secretary's voice

Yes.......I'll see if he has time to speak
with you.

There is a brief silence, then secretary's voice
again.

Secretary

I'm sorry, Mr. Alexander. Mr. Short said
he cannot get
involved with your situation.

Don looks at phone, then hangs up with a belly
laugh. He steps outside the booth, looks back

toward Roman's courtroom, and walks the other way.

INT. LAW SCHOOL LIBRARY – DAY

Don walks from book shelves with armload of law books, unloads onto table, then returns to shelves and retrieves another armload. When he returns, Harry is seated at table. Don dumps books onto table, grins at Harry and sits down.

Don

Sneaked right up on me.......did you?

Harry

I spied you hustling books.......I came over to help you read and take notes. Maybe we'll get outta here in time to get a pizza......if we find what you're looking for before midnight.

Don

We're looking for any federal procedural rules peculiar to allegations of a conspiracy to violate civil rights, and immunity defenses for judges dodging civil damages who are involved in the conspiracy and charged by a federal prosecutor......and proper service of subpoenas upon judges to force them to testify concerning crimes committed in their courtrooms. That should keep us busy until they lock the doors tonight.

Harry lets out a hearty chuckle and helps sort the law books.

Harry

What did Judge Roman say?

Don

He'll testify if I subpoena him.

INT. WALTER NEWBURG'S OFFICE – NIGHT

Walter Newburg   is sitting at desk drinking cocktail and smoking cigarette. The ornate wall clock to the right of desk reads 8:22 pm. The desk phone rings. Walter punches a button activating speaker on desk phone.

Walter

Walter Newburg....

Voice on phone

Dale Conley, Walter....sorry to be so late getting back to you, but I wanted to make sure we're clear with the Missouri Supreme Court

before you draft your opinion.

Walter

Are they with us?

Voice on phone

No sweat....we can deny his discovery

efforts and the majority of justices will back us if

he appeals.

Walter replies with relieved tone.

Walter

That's great news. I'll deny his request on

the basis that the state records are not relevant to

the issues to be ruled on be me.

Voice on phone

The Supreme Court will only hear the record produced before you.....so that allows you to control what Alexander can argue on appeal.....and the justices will set a limit of ten minutes on his oral argument.

Walter

That about covers things for now......see you at the hearing.

INT. DANNY'S APARTMENT – NIGHT

Don and Danny sit at kitchen table playing chess and discussing legal issues.

Danny

It appears to me that you're pissing into the wind, Dad. Those who make and enforce the law are the same people who break the law with impunity. When the lawmakers become the law

breakers, who do you turn to?

Don

The only solution when dealing with
absolute power is the knife and gun. You can
search six thousand years of human history and
not find a single instance where absolute power
yielded to reason or legal restraints.

Danny

You're not going to kill anyone, Dad. I
know you too well to believe otherwise. You
cannot prevent crime by becoming a criminal.

Don

To be guilty of committing a crime, both
intent and at least one overt act must be proven.
Intent may be demonstrated by act or speech. An

overt act by definition is doing something to carry out the demonstrated intent. A threat of illegal violence is no more than idle free speech when spoken or written in a public forum in the absence of an overt act.

Danny

Does that mean what I think you just said? You might focus public attention on corrupt lawyers and judges by publicly threatening some sort of violence?

Don

I might if left no other choice.

INT. PROFESSOR'S LEVINE'S CLASSROOM

Levine stands at podium winding up a lecture on professional ethics.

Levine

...........moreover, members of the Bar

must avoid even the appearance of impropriety

in order to maintain public trust.

Don and Harry are seated next to each other near center of classroom. They exchange looks of total disdain as Levine continues.

Levine

As officers of the court, we are bound by

the public trust to conduct ourselves in

accordance with the strict standards of our

profession. That concludes our final ethics

lecture. Don't forget to arrive one half hour

before graduation ceremonies.

Students gather up books and pads and head for exits. Don and Harry walk toward front exit door.

Harry

What a two-faced pretender! If I had to listen to any more, I'd puke!

Don

I believe it was the prophet, Jeremiah, who said: "The heart of man is deceitful above all things and desperately wicked."

Don and Harry pause in hallway outside classroom.

Don

I'm going to hang back and challenge him.

Harry

Be gentle.....he's got his career and judgeship on the line.

Harry moves away and Don waits for Levine to exit classroom.

Levine gathers up his lecture materials and exits classroom. He sees Don waiting in hallway.

Don

Got a minute, Professor?

Levine

Walk with me to the elevator.

Don and Levine begin walking down hallway toward elevator.

Don

How does it make you feel, Jim, to lecture on morals and ethics while knowing exactly what's going on in Missouri's legal system?

Levine looks around to see if anybody is in earshot.

Levine

I'm a tenured professor with a family to support.....including two boys starting college.

Don and Levine have reached the elevator and are standing in front of the door.

Don

And.....it makes you nervous to be seen with me?

Levine answers in a cracking voice.

I was called at home and threatened.....Dean Henz called me and relayed a direct threat from Roland Sanford.

Don exhibits a look of astonishment.

Don

Sandford! The president of the Law Board!! Mr. Ethics himself? That would nail him as acting in furtherance of a civil rights conspiracy and willful interference with my right to counsel.

Levine eyes are now glistening with tears.

Levine

It upset me very much. I even discussed it with my wife. I considered telling Henz and Sandford to take a hike. They think I'm helping you plead your case......and threatened me on behalf the Law Board, Missouri Bar, and some other very powerful individuals.

The elevator doors open and several students exit; two wait to speak to Levine.

Don

*Thanks, Professor.....I was a little confused
on that case law.*

Don turns and walks toward the main entrance.

INT. JUDGE ORVILLE WHITE'S CHAMBERS
– EARLY EVENING

White sits at desk and Roland sits in plain chair across from him. Brass name tag identifies White. The wall clock reads 6:47 pm. White leans back in his swivel chair and taps fingers together. He addresses Roland in a knowing voice.

Judge White

*So, you denied Alexander permission to
sit for the bar exam because he caught Simon
and Dixon filing a false affidavit and backdating*

a court document.....and figured he'd come

crawling to you with hat in hand begging

permission to sit for the bar exam.

Roland

It's true. We entirely misjudged the man.

Judge White

I see......rather than abase himself, he

chose to sue everyone involved for conspiracy to

violate his civil rights......a federal felony, not to

mention double perjury in the court

record......which he has a certified copy of.....and

so does Sam Biden.

Roland appears very uncomfortable and speaks in
fawning voice.

Roland

The Law Board is entitled to the same immunity from civil suits as all other Missouri Supreme Court appointees serving in state administrative offices. The criminal complaint is a separate issue which Sam will elect to ignore as a frivolous waste of federal funds......which is well within his legal discretion.

Judge White

You'd better review federal case law on both issues......like Forrester v. White and Hoover v. Ronwin.....and pray fervently that Alexander can't find a greedy out-of-state lawyer who has credentials to practice before the federal bench.....and Sam Biden better study up on available defenses to malfeasance and dereliction of duty.

Roland

No one in the Missouri Bar will take his case. Out-of-state counsel is not going to pay much attention to a case branded as frivolous with a ten thousand dollars fine. I doubt if the Eighth Circuit will even bother to read his appeal......if he files one.

Judge White remains silent for a few moments and drums his fingers lightly on his desktop. He squints at Roland with ambiguous look.

Judge White

What were those donkeys at Simon and Dixon thinking about when they started jerking this guy around. You'd better hire some extra security. When Alexander gets his belly full, you felons are gonna need protecting.

Roland

I know we all stepped in it, Your Honor.....we should have let Simon and Dixon bail themselves out of their own perjury. I guess we're in your hands.

Judge White

You may be beyond help. Alexander is not an ass kisser nor driven by political ambition. You have helped AMI steal five and a half million from him. You have shit all over him because you hold the power to do so and he knows you are guilty of multiple felonies. He is divorced and his children are intelligent adults. He is 51 and you have destroyed his old age security. I suggest round the clock body guards.

Roland

Maybe so, Your Honor, but we can't undo what is on the record.

Judge White

Your private investigator reports that
Alexander's son is going to medical school and
that his daughter is going to nursing school.
Maybe he'll want to see his grandchildren more
than retribution on you jackasses

Roland

Your Honor, you know you have our full
support and funding when a seat opens up in the
Eighth Circuit.

White stares at Roland and shakes his head with
disappointment.

Judge White

I'll have my clerk draft a wordy judgment
to muddy up the water....and I'll hit him with the
maximum fine. You are correct. The Circuit

bench won't read beyond my clerk's lengthy

citations.

Roland flashes a grateful smile.

Roland

The ten thousand dollars fine should

discourage an appeal to the Circuit

for fear of additional sanctions.

Judge White

If I say he's wasting the court's time, no

one will overrule me on the facts. I am the

ultimate trier of facts in my court. On points of

law......who is going to listen to a pro se plaintiff

already sanctioned by a federal judge?

EXT. LOCAL PUBLIC PARK WITH SMALL
FISHING LAKE – DAY

Under clear, sunny sky, Don and Lee relax in a small fishing boat near tree sheltered shoreline. Lee jerks the tip of her fishing rod upward and hooks a fish. She begins reeling the fish in and Don picks up dip net from inside bottom of boat.

Don

Looks like a nice one, Honey.....keep your rod tip up and bring it in slow. I'll net it for you.

Lee plays the fish while Don watches with anticipation and admiring smile. Lee squeals with excitement.

Lee

Feels like a big catfish.....

Don

It's coming up....I can see it....

Lee keeps rod tip up and continues reeling in the fish. A nice sized catfish breaks the water surface. Don nets the fish

Don

All right! Time for lunch.

EXT. SHADED PARK AREA WITH PICNIC TABLE AND GRILL – DAY

Don and Lee sit at table set with thermos, cups, plastic utensils, paper plates and napkins. Smoke rises from the fish cooking on grill.

Don

It was a setup.....no doubt about it. The surrogate and his attorney focused on my complaints against the Law Board members and my suit in federal court.

Lee

How can they get by with that. They
assured you by personal letters that those issues
wouldn't be aired at the hearing.

Don sips coffee from paper cup, sets cup down
and gazes back at Lee with expression of
revulsion.

Don

The letters served to set me up.....not only
to deny me access to state records, but also to
trap me into a hearing with no hard evidence
pertaining to issues being argued on the record.

Lee

And, the appellate judges would not
consider the letters because they were omitted

from the official record forwarded to the court by
the surrogate.

Don

You got it....doesn't matter that it was
dishonest, immoral and highly unethical. The
surrogate's plan was simply to control the record
being considered on appeal. And, I didn't see it
coming.

Lee looks bewildered.

Lee

But....the Missouri Supreme Court justices
saw the letters.....they were included in your brief
filed with the clerk.

Don looks pensive, as if trying to put his finger on some missing link. He pulls pen and small pad from shirt pocket and scribbles some notes.

Lee watches with anticipation and sips her drink.

Don

The justices saw the letters......if they read my brief. Think about that for a minute. If they didn't read my brief, they are guilty of gross judicial misconduct.....if they did read it......then, they're guilty of acting in furtherance of an exposed conspiracy to omit a critical portion of the record on appeal......knowingly and maliciously.

Lee

I don't quite follow your reasoning.

Don

*It's judicial misconduct for any judge to
issue a ruling on appeal without considering the
points of law raised by both sides.....and that's
mighty hard to do if the appellant's brief is not
even read......especially in the absence of oral
argument.*

Lee

*And.....you waived oral argument fifteen
days before
the actual court hearing.*

Don

*Yes.....over my written objections, and with
no explanation whatsoever, the justices reduced
my time for oral argument from forty minutes
down to just ten minutes......forcing me to either
waive oral argument or fall flat on my face*

before the bench trying to present a coherent

summary.

Lee

Apparently, the rule of law doesn't count for much.

Don

Remember my writ of mandamus? I handed it to the appellate clerk at around 3:30 pm, and the rejection notice to me was typed the same day. The court closed at 5:00 pm. The writ was a seventy page document. The appellate judges never had time to read the writ.....much less meet and discuss the points of law, then vote and render a decision. The problem is that I had no way to prove that. The clerk would just claim she made a mistake regarding the date when typing the notice.

Lee chokes up with anger.

Lee

They should all be in prison.....

Don

*All the judges involved knew precisely
what was going down....but I need more evidence
to convince a jury.*

INT. EXCLUSIVE RESTAURANT – EVENING

White coated waiter carries tray of drinks to very private table in rear of dining room. Herman Dixon and Henry Magene are seated at table conversing confidentially over empty drinks. As waiter serves fresh drinks, they pause their conversation and Herman looks toward front for their expected guests.

Henry

Thank you, John. We will wait to order until our guests arrive.

John nods okay, picks up the empty glasses and heads back toward bar. Henry leans toward Herman confidentially.

Henry

It's already assigned out. Pippen and Baker are on the three-judge panel which will hear the appeal.

Herman

Excellent! We played a major role in their appointment to the Circuit bench.....they owe us big time. That's two votes on the panel....enough to boot Alexander.

Henry

That will certainly kill his final appeal. The U.S. Supreme Court has never granted a hearing after both the District Court and the Eighth Circuit Court of Appeals have dismissed the case as frivolous.

John shows Frank Pippen and Howard Baker to Simon and Dixon's table.

John

It's right back here in our private section.....may I bring you something to drink, Gentlemen?

Pippen

Manhattan....

Baker

Johnny Walker Red.....on the rocks.

Herman and Henry rise from table to greet Pippen and Baker. John heads to bar to get more drinks. Herman and Henry fawningly shake hands with the judges while orally greeting them.

Herman

Good evening, Your Honors....we're very pleased you could come.....we were getting a bit worried.

Herman and Henry pull out well padded chairs for their esteemed guests.

Baker

No need to worry.....we got stuck in traffic.

Pippen

*No way we're going to pass up free drinks
and dinner at this place......you fellows must be
rolling in cash.*

Herman

*We got a little head start.....what's
your pleasure?*

Herman lights up a cigarette.

Pippen

*We're all set......the waiter took our
order when we came in.*

John approaches table with drinks ordered by
judges and fresh drinks for Herman and Henry.

John

I'll make sure you gentlemen don't run dry. Just give me a nod when you're ready to order.

The table is silent until John moves away. Then, Baker raises his glass somberly.

Baker

Here's to a few minutes of sticky business.....then on to gourmet dining with pleasant company....

The other three touch glasses with Baker.

Herman and Henry jointly

Hear! Hear!

Baker lowers glass to table, and locks his fingertips. He displays a poker face.

Baker

I suppose it has occurred to you that your strategy in Alexander's litigation has been less than clever......

Henry and Herman adopt a kiss ass countenance.

Herman

A point well taken.....and a mistake we shall not repeat.

Henry coughs to relieve tension and Herman stubs out his cigarette.

Pippen

Nevertheless, the matter will be quietly laid to rest. His appeal will be dismissed as frivolous......with no response to his legal

argument.

Baker concurs in the illegal conspiracy.

Baker

We'll fine him double costs to impress

upon the high court

that his claim is without merit.

Herman

It's a sure bet he'll appeal all the way to

the U.S. Supreme Court regardless of the fines

and sanctions.

Pippen dismisses further appeal with superior tone.

Pippen

The nine wise ones in Washington will not hear a litigant whose case has twice been judged frivolous in both law and fact.......end of business now. Let's move on to things more pleasant.

INT. PROFESSOR LEVINE'S OFFICE – DAY

Levine is rocked back in his chair behind his desk gazing at ceiling. Don sits across from him. Don's face shows barely controlled rage. Levine rocks back to level position and folds arms over his chest. Don waits for Levine's opinion on recent developments. Levine's demeanor reveals puzzled insecurity.

Levine

The entire scenario is awfully fishy.....none of us understands how your case can legally be dismissed as frivolous.

111

Don

White's ruling directly contradicts constitutional law, statutory law and case law......not to mention basic common sense.

Levine nods in agreement.

Levine

No question about that. Your case was well stated, supported by numerous U.S. Supreme Court decisions, federal statutory law....and certainly was not frivolous. The only explanation is a civil rights conspiracy involving a lot of Bar members.

Don's voice is husky with rage.

Don

The dishonest, immoral, unethical, gutless,

hypocrites are trying to discredit my appeal!

Levine appears to be taken back somewhat by the sheer force of Don's anger.

Levine

The jury will have to hold their noses ....if

you can ever get

past the legal fraternity.

Don's voice drips with contempt.

Don

If these legal whores think this fight is

over they sorely misjudged me.

Levine replies in supportive tone.

Levine

The law clearly entitles you to a trial before your peers in that your case is obviously well grounded in law and fact......but you are fighting a powerful and tightly knit legal brotherhood that controls our legal system in Missouri.

Don

Perhaps it is time to replace the pen with the sword.

Levine

You're effectively barred from the courts. The judges are personal friends with the lawyers you're accusing.......friends who put them on the bench. No judge in this state is going to buck the Law Board, the Missouri Bar, and the Missouri Supreme Court justices.

Don

I've got to find a way to get the
media involved.

Levine looks at floor and shrugs apologetically.

Levine

I've got my family to think about.

Don's anger boils over.

Don

Exactly!! That's why they're able to get by
with just about anything. Self policing
profession!! What a sick joke.

Give the system a chance to work at the higher level of justice. The United States Supreme Court hasn't turned you down.

Don

They will......the frivolous label will quash my appeal. None of the   justices will bother to even read my brief.

INT. DON'S APARTMENT – DAY

Danny is sitting at kitchen table adjacent to living room about fifteen feet from entry door. Between kitchen and living room is a large walk through which allows partial view of both kitchen and living room. Danny is drinking coffee and reading newspaper. Don enters kitchen through living room, pitches four open letters onto table and pours himself a cup of coffee.

Danny

More bad news?

Don wrestles with himself to subdue his temper. His rage seething below the surface of borderline self-control is obvious. His voice is hard as flint.

Don

Both the Missouri Supreme Court and the U.S. Supreme Court basically ignored me. The Missouri bench rejected my administrative appeal; and the federal bench refused to hear my appeal on the civil suit. The federal prosecutor used his legal discretion and refused to initiate an investigation into my criminal complaint. I have now been all the way through

both the state and federal court systems, and
never once had the opportunity to present
evidence to support my complaints.

Danny responds in an exasperated voice.

Danny
So.......what are you going to do next?

Don
I'm going to file a motion for rehearing in
the Eighth Circuit and argue self-defense since
I'm being denied legal recourse.

INT. PIZZA HUT – NOON

Don and Lee sit at table eating pizza and drinking cokes. Both appear quiet and reflective. Lee finishes a slice of pizza and sips her coke. Don

also finishes a slice and washes it down with soda.
Don gazes at Lee pensively.

Don:

Are you able to keep up with your classes?

Lee

I'm only working twenty hours each week.
The old jalopy is working out, so I'm okay. I
really don't need any thing else.

Don

That's good, because my incentive
earnings will never be paid. I'm just tilting at
windmills in the courts.

Lee shakes her head sadly and finishes the last of
her pizza and coke. She pushes back from table,

kisses Don on cheek, and gathers up her purse and books.

Lee

I gotta run, Dad........don't worry about me.

INT. LAW SCHOOL MAIN LOBBY – DAY

Students are ambling about the lobby areas; Don stands at lobby elevator waiting.

Elevator doors open. Don gets in, doors close. Elevator rises to second floor, doors open, Don exits and walks down hall to Professor Levine's office. The door is open. Don looks inside and sees that Levine is not in office. Don walks back toward elevator and goes into restroom. He squats down and looks for feet in stalls. No one is around. He stands in front of sink mirror, lifts shirt tail and removes small tape recorder from waist band of his jeans. He clicks off recorder, rewinds tape and sticks recorder back into place. He uses urinal, washes hands, and fluffs out shirt; then exits restroom and walks back down hall to Levine's office. The door is still open and Levine sits at his desk working at computer.

Don taps on door post. Levine looks up from computer.

Levine

Hi, Don...come on in.....be with you in a moment.

Don enters office and sits down in chair opposite desk. Levine makes few more keyboard entries and then swivels to face Don.

Don

Maybe I'd better close the door.....

Don gets up, closes door and sits down again.

Levine

*What's going on with you?.....haven't seen
you since graduation. Got any plans I can help
you with?......references, written
recommendations, etc.?*

Don

*I appreciate your offer, but there's
nothing you can do. My administrative appeal
got turned down by the Missouri Supreme Court;
and the U.S. Supreme Court refused to hear my
appeal from the Eighth Circuit.*

Levine

Were you allowed oral argument before
the Eighth Circuit?

Don

No.......I have not had an actual court
hearing since being fed to Simon and Dixon's
pet judge in the St. Louis City equity division.

Levine rocks back in chair and folds arms across
chest while looking at ceiling.

Levine

And, all your procedural objections
were summarily denied?

Don's voice if flat and without emotion.

Don

Yes....without being read.

Don squints at Levin.

Don

Let me ask you a moot question, Jim. How do you feel when reflecting upon the president of the Law Board threatening the dean of the law school to interfere with my access to legal counsel? Wasn't that just a wee bit unethical?

Levine

Yes.....no question about it.....also a criminal act.

Don

I'm disappointed in Dean Henz......that he bowed to the threat.

Levine replies in confessing voice.

Levine

I was flabbergasted when he called me at home and relayed the threat to my career as well as careers of other members of the faculty.

Don

Isn't intentional interference with the right to counsel a federal felony in itself. Perhaps I should proceed with a separate criminal complaint and civil suit. Interference with counsel is a separate criminal act apart from the conspiracy complaint. All I need is some hard evidence to support my new case......and every faculty member knows about the threat from

Roland Sanford to blackball any member of the

Missouri Bar who assists me.

Levine answers in uncertain, stuttering voice.

Er...er...when it comes.....ah.....ah....to

getting such admissions on the

record.....ah......nobody will admit what we

heard.....and....we do know that certain

statements have been made in a roundabout

manner....ah......er.

Don continues to press Levine.

Don

Doesn't every member of the Missouri

Bar swear an oath to report ethics violations

which they become aware of? Is the entire

faculty lacking integrity such that their oath

means absolutely nothing?

Levine

That....ah....ah.....might be a little overstated.

Don tone reflects total disgust.

Don

I think not......would you like to hear a replay of your own admissions?

Don lifts shirt tail and exposes tape recorder.

Don

Don't worry Jim, just tell the bad guys that I taped this conversation without your knowledge. You didn't rat on them.

INT. EXCLUSIVE COUNTRY CLUB DINING ROOM – DAY

Members are scattered around tables drinking and talking to each other.

Mary Totten sits at a table reading legal documents and taking notes while sipping a cocktail. She keeps an eye on the side entrance door. Roland Sanford, Sam Biden, and Henry Mageen drive up to side entrance of dining room and exit their golf carts. The three men are laughing and joking with each other.

Henry

Hey....Sam.....you might be a fine U.S. Attorney but you can sure use some golf lessons.

Roland

Don't be too hard on Sam..... he's got some other assets.

The three men enter club dining room and continue the banter.

Sam

My wife could out golf you two.....

Roland

I bet your wife wouldn't know a nine iron from a putter.

Henry

Shhhhh.......watch your mouth.   There's Mary......she can out golf us all.

The three men gather around Mary's table. She looks up from her notes and smiles.

Mary

*Hi, Guys. Finally get nine holes in, or
did you take a nap?*

Sam

*Be nice, Mary. They've had a pretty
tough outing....*

While laughing at each other, the men pull up
chairs and join Mary.

Mary glances at her watch.

Mary

*You guys burned up my time shagging
balls outta the woods. I've got to leave in five
minutes.....so let's get down to business.
Alexander has a tape recording wherein
Professor Levine makes some admissions that*

could incriminate us all and support a criminal

complaint.

Sam

I've heard all about it. He will have to file

his complaint with me and needless to say, I

simply won't waste my federal funds chasing

after frivolous charges by some obviously

paranoid law student unfit to practice law....and

Judge White will not entertain another civil suit

so we really don't have a problem.

Mary drinks bottom of her cocktail.

Mary

That's all we need to hear, Sam. We won't

forget your cooperation.

Sam calls out in boisterous tone.

131

Sam

Hey!....waiter. How bout some drinks over here?

INT. KITCHEN IN DON'S APARTMENT – MORNING

Don and Danny are enjoying breakfast together. Bacon, eggs, toast, coffee and jelly are visible. Danny sips coffee with puzzled expression.

Danny

Why wouldn't the U.S. Attorney at least

investigate your

complaint?   I guess I'm missing something.

Don

All prosecutors, both state and federal,

have wide discretion as to whose complaint gets

investigated and whose doesn't. Their budget isn't unlimited. They get to choose, within limited parameters, how their funds are spent. Such discretion allows them to repay political favors within the brotherhood.

Don and Danny resume eating and Danny appears to ponder Don's explanation.

Danny

You mean they can let off anybody they choose?

Don

That's true as long as there is no public outcry....and the public doesn't care about my case because the media has not raised the question of dereliction of duty. The articles that

were published have painted me as some kind of
legal jerk. The local media depends on the
system for inside information; and the national
media cannot see any more than procedural
wrangling between a misfit and the Missouri
Bar.

Danny is mystified.

Danny

So, what recourse do you have?

Don

I'm going to file a petition for rehearing before
the U.S. Court of Appeals for the Eighth Circuit
based upon Levine's taped admission.

Danny

What good will that do? They will ignore
you again.

Don

The media will cover this pleading because
I'm going to argue self-defense.

Danny

Self defense? I don't follow your logic.

Don:

I'll argue that since the courts have barred
their doors to me, and the U.S. Attorney refuses
to investigate my complaint of numerous felonies
being perpetrated against me, I have the right to
defend myself with deadly force.

Danny

You mean you're going to threaten to kill some
people? Can't you be arrested for that?

Don

Not as long as it's just rhetoric and I don't actually try to hurt anybody. I am asking a legal question......if the law doesn't apply to me, then I am not bound by the law and thus entitled to act in self-defense. Moreover, my statements will be in a legal pleading submitted to a court of law......and all such legal arguments, however unsavory, are absolutely immune from either civil or criminal liability.

Danny

So, in effect, you're telling the judges to honor your constitutional rights to due process and equal protection of the laws......or suffer total exposure of their malfeasance in office when you defend yourself against homicide charges.

Don:

That's the logic of my plan....and should get the media to asking the right questions, and perhaps focusing public attention on the corruption within the Missouri Bar.

Danny

Sounds like it just might work.

INT. LAW OFFICE OF NORMAN PRATT – MORNING

Norman sits at his desk talking on phone to Paula Vaughn. His desk is littered with legal papers.

Norman

No.....it came in the morning mail certified to all attorneys of record.

Paula on phone

You know more about his thinking than any of us on the Bar Committee, having worked with the private detective....are we in any real danger?

Norman

No....Paula. He's just trying to get some media attention. We've got to find a way to shut him up before the media takes him seriously and he winds up on television asking a lot of very embarrassing questions.

Paula on phone

Why don't Rachael and I complain to Susan Wright and get him arrested on the grounds that he has frightened us with his threats.

Norman

On what legal basis? He hasn't communicated any threats outside of the Eighth Circuit Court of Appeals......and what he argues is protected by the first amendment freedom of speech as well as the absolute immunity which attaches to all legal pleadings.

Paula on phone

Susan Wright will cooperate. She'll dust off the books and come up with something that will satisfy her boss in county prosecution. Judge

Schepler is due to get the next criminal case and she owes us for persuading the governor to favor her appointment to the bench.

Norman

Judy Schepler is a flaming novice who can barely find her way to her own chambers. She'll be a pushover for the prosecution......go for it, Paula.

EXT. APARTMENT COMPLEX – EARLY EVENING

Three Columbia police cars pull up to Don's apartment. The drivers exit and gather outside Don's entry door. One cop raps loudly on door. Don opens door. The cop who knocked steps into Don's apartment and the other two block the door. Cop in apartment addresses Don in curt tone.

Cop

Are You Donald Alexander?

Don

I certainly am....why are you here?

Cop

*You're under arrest on two
counts of harassment.*

Don

Why am I not surprised?

Don steps outside door. The cop inside steps out while Don locks door and then submits to handcuffing.

Don

Don't bother rattling off my non-existent rights. I'm not only an ex- cop; I also have a law degree. Let's get on with this fiasco.

INT. PUBLIC DEFENDER'S OFFICE, COLUMBIA MISSOURI – DAY

The office is small, shabby, dirty and extremely cluttered. A young, long-haired public defender wearing unkept suit sits behind a battered metal desk. Don sits in a scarred up metal chair across from him. The hand written name tag taped to front of desk reads Bret Heinze. Bret grins like a possum.

                    Bret
You ain't exactly popular with the Missouri Bar.

                    Don

They didn't exactly get in line to snap up my case.....but, since I'm broke anyway, I lucked out and got you.

Bret

*I've already been threatened by the
prosecution....said they wanted to get you for
political reasons and strongly recommended that
I not get in their way. They threatened to not
plea bargain with me and to bury me in
paperwork.*

Don

*And, of course, you told them to take
their threats and shove 'em......that the only
things might scare you are rattlesnakes
hanging from their belly buttons.*

Bret snickers and avoids Don's gaze.

Bret

*Not exactly. Just thought you should
know about the threat.*

Don

I don't suppose you'd like to admit being threatened by the prosecution to the media?

Bret appears somewhat amused.

Bret

No.....and I'll deny it if asked by anyone but you. I'm your lawyer.....not your friend. I don't wanna be sitting where you are.

Don

Now that we both understand you're cowed by the prosecution, what is your defense strategy? Maybe I can help draft the pretrial pleadings.

Bret rocks back in chair and props feet on his desk.

Bret

Free speech.....immunity of legal pleadings.....and the information charged does not constitute an offense under the language of Revised Missouri Statute 565.090.....the statute under which you are charged with two counts of harassment.

Don

RSMO 565.090 is aimed at preventing harassing telephone calls and hate mail directed to Missouri citizens within the privacy of their own homes, not free speech in a public forum......and certainly cannot be construed as superseding the absolute privilege which attaches to every legal pleading. This charge against me is either issued by a legal idiot or is already bought off by the assigned judge. The jury would then only be allowed to consider whether I actually scared two poor little old ladies who just happen to be truly kind hearted, public spirited, hard working lawyers dedicated to enforcing law and order.

Bret scratches his chin with his right hand and chuckles.

Bret

They want to stick you with a conviction to discredit you in the eyes of the general public. Nobody pays attention to convicted criminals.....certainly not the appellate courts in Missouri.....the actual hidden backbone of the legal fraternity you're fighting.......a losing battle I can assure you. The prosecution holds all the cards.

Don

If you like, I'll draft the motion to dismiss, and prepare our futile notice of appeal. I can also help with the research for needed case citations.

Bret

I'll take all the help you can give me......I'm swamped.

INT. COURTROOM – DAY

The courtroom is half filled with criminal defendants and their lawyers. An armed bailiff stands to left of bench. The brass name plate on right corner of bench reads Honorable Judy Schepler. She is young, attractive and fumbling. A prisoner in an orange jumpsuit and his attorney stand at bench. Schepler is making notes on the cover of the case file.

Judge Schepler

The motion for bail is granted......five thousand dollars.......next case.

Bailiff picks up file folder from table next to his guard position and calls next case.

Bailiff

State of Missouri versus Donald Alexander......case number 31839M....

Don, Bret and Susan Wright arise and walk to front of bench.

Schepler rattles on in bored monotone.

Judge Schepler

Defendant appears in person and with counsel. Susan Wright appears for the state. Defendant is charged with two counts of

harassment in violation of Revised Missouri
Statute 565.090. Do you wish to argue
defendant's motion to dismiss, Mr. Heinze?

Bret:

Yes, Your Honor. Mr. Alexander is
charged with harassment as set forth under
statute 565.090 in connection with a legal
pleading which he filed in the United States
Court of Appeals for the Eighth Circuit.....a
motion for rehearing. Over fifty years of case law
which is certainly binding upon this court
provides absolute immunity for all legal
pleadings. Moreover, Mr. Alexander's written
statements were directed to a court of law and
not to the alleged victims.....Paula Vaughn and
Rachael Phelps. Statute 565.090 prohibits only
direct phone or personal mail communications
directed to a citizen in the privacy of his/her

home for the purpose of obvious harassment.
The information charged does not even allege
that Mr. Alexander sent personal mail to, or
telephoned, either Ms. Vaughn or Ms. Phelps.
Therefore the two counts of harassment are non-
existent in both law and fact and must be
forthwith dismissed.

Schepler appears totally bored and picks at her fingernails.

Judge Schepler

Argument for the state, Ms. Wright?

Susan

Yes, Your Honor. It is not required that
the intended victim actually receive the threat in
person. The victims here became aware of the
threat when a copy of the pleading filed in the
Eighth Circuit was mailed to all attorneys of

record who obviously were justified in fearing for their lives. The question of intent to harass is a jury issue and is not to be determined in a pretrial hearing.

Bret

Your Honor, Ms. Wright is rewriting the statute to suit her own purpose. She is grossly misquoting the language of 565.090 which absolutely requires direct personal communication to the alleged victim by telephone or hate mail.

Bret hands a copy of statute to Bailiff. Bailiff hands copy to Schepler as Bret continues:

Bret

Moreover, Your Honor, statutory, procedural and case law does not permit

properly submitted legal pleading to be classified
as hate mail.

Schepler appears somewhat unsure of herself. She fumbles with the copy of the Missouri statute and then lays it aside.

Judge Schepler

Defendant's motion to dismiss is overruled. Trial is set for April 22nd at nine o'clock. Call the next case......

INT. CONFERENCE ROOM IN PROSECUTOR'S OFFICE – MORNING

The conference room contains a round table with seating for eight. There is water and coffee service plus platter of donuts. Harry Meeks, Paula Vaughn, Rachael Phelps and Susan Wright are drinking coffee and eating donuts. Harry finishes off a donut, sips coffee and rattles spoon against a water glass.

Harry

Okay......let's move along. I've got about twenty minutes before I meet with Judge Schepler. My opinion is that any conviction of Alexander based on RSMo 565.090 will be reversed on appeal. Since Alexander was arrested, jailed and posted bond, based solely on Susan's idiotic reading of the statute, we will be lucky if we're not sued for false arrest, false imprisonment, and malicious prosecution......because that is precisely what we are guilty of. Unfortunately, this arrest warrant was issued without notifying me. I discussed this stupidity with the Cole County Prosecutor and he agrees totally with my analysis that the charges against Alexander are absolutely unconstitutional.

Susan reacts with cocky confidence.

                          Susan

    Schepler has already overruled his motion
    to dismiss, so he's going to the jury who only
    hears questions of fact, not law. We'll get a
    conviction that will stick because Alexander has
    burned all his bridges behind him. The appellate
    courts, both state and federal, have given him the
    boot and will consider any future appeal by him
    as frivolous. The reason we need this conviction
    is to discredit him when he wheedles to the
    media. Don't worry, Harry, your conviction
    record won't be tarnished.

Harry pulls notes from his folder and continues
with obvious concern.

Susan looks around at the others with a superior smirk.

Harry

Alexander is already making waves with the press. In a statement delivered early this morning to all local media he stated: "It is patently obvious to anyone with common sense that Harry Meeks, Boone County Prosecutor, Susan Wright, his assistant, alleged victims Paula Vaughn and Rachael Phelps, and newly appointed Judge Judy Schepler have illegally conspired to have me arrested and prosecuted based on a non-existent statutory prohibition which the prosecution declares overturns constitutional law and the absolute immunity which attaches to every legal pleading filed in a court of law. The prosecution is illegal, malicious and carried out solely in retribution against me for trying to expose gross

155

malfeasance in office constituting federal

felonies on the part of prominent members of the

Missouri Bar association."

Harry lays copy of Don's press release on table and looks around at attendees.

Harry

I don't think you ladies will like federal

prison. I hereby wash my hands completely of

this entire matter and will present Judge

Schepler with my sworn statement that the arrest

warrant for Alexander was issued in my absence,

without my permission, and is absolutely

unfounded in law and fact. The criminal liability

for this conspiracy rests on your shoulders.

The conspiracy has been carried out, the false

arrest, false imprisonment and malicious

prosecution are too far along to simply drop

charges. The damage has been done, the liability

is established and cannot be erased by moronic

excuses.

Harry picks up his folder and exits the conference room

INT. PUBLIC DEFENDER'S OFFICE -- DAY

Don and Bret are sitting at Bret's desk drinking coffee and filling out subpoenas.

                    Bret
Do you think Judge Roman will actually testify.

                    Don
He said he would if subpoenaed.....and I
believe he has integrity.

Bret

The only witnesses you can call are
lawyers and judges. I'm sure that the prosecution
will file a motion to quash your subpoenas and
Schepler will accommodate them.

Don

No doubt, but we'll issue them and get them
on the record.

Bret

Once we concede that Schepler will force
you to trial after quashing your subpoenas, the
only defense we can turn to is that you were
merely trying to get the attention of the Eighth
Circuit judges with zero intent to harass the
alleged victims.

Don

When the prosecution gets me in front of a jury, I'll be guilty until proven innocent. They'll naturally assume that my intent was to scare a couple of older women just as the warrant charges. The public clings to the illusion that the police won't arrest you unless you have violated the law.

Bret

After Schepler quashes your subpoenas, the prosecution will argue that your testimony is self-serving and not to be believed. The little ole ladies will cry crocodile tears about being really terrified.

Don

That's the problem with being forced into a jury trial in spite of immunity and constitutional guarantees. The only question the jury will decide is whether I had the intent to harass Vaughn and Phelps.....and their answer will be a resounding "yes."

INT. COURTROOM – MID-MORNING

Susan and Bret are standing at bench. Don is sitting in front row.

Schepler is ruling on the prosecution's motion to quash Don's subpoenas for defense witnesses.

Bret
Your Honor, the only defense the court has allowed my client is that he had no intent to harass a couple of hardened lawyers who are not afraid to perjure themselves before this court.

How can he support that defense after you quash

his subpoenas? You would not be permitting

him to present any corroborating testimony.

Under due process, he has the absolute right to

subpoena any witness who can give testimony

concerning the issue of intent. The trial will be

unconstitutional, a legal farce, and without

parallel in the entire history of American

jurisprudence.

Schepler is again picking at her nails.

Judge Schepler
I am inclined to agree with the prosecution

that the testimony to be elicited from your list of

subpoenaed witnesses is not relevant to the

question of intent. The prosecution's motion is

therefore sustained.

INT. PUBLIC DEFENDER'S OFFICE –
EARLY EVENING

Don and Bret are eating a pizza and sipping cokes.

Don

*I wonder how Schepler got appointed to
the bench. Do you think she actually
graduated from law school?*

Bret

*Judicial competence is not required to
become a judge in Missouri. You just have to be
admitted to the brotherhood.*

Don

*I suspect the same holds true for American
jurisprudence.*

Bret

Well.....we might as well start drafting an appellate brief because you are definitely going to get convicted of harassment.

INT. COURTROOM – DAY

The twelve jurors, eight of which are women, have returned to the jury box following deliberation. Don, Bret and Susan sit at opposing counsel tables. The jurors display deadpan expressions.

Schepler addressed the jury in a monotone voice.

Judge Schepler

Ladies and Gentlemen of the jury.....have you reached a verdict?

The female juror in seat number one rises to her feet.

Jury foreperson

Yes, Your Honor........we, the jury, find the defendant guilty as charged.

Bret

Three cheers for the red, white and blue.

Don

Post-trial motions and appeals will be a total waste of time seeing that the entire Missouri Bar is locking arms to protect itself. However, motions and appeals will keep me out of the slammer for several months. Go ahead and file an appeal Bret. I've got a few things to take care of. I might not see you for awhile.

INT. DON'S APARTMENT – LATE MORNING

Don sits at kitchen table. A duffel bag is in center of table. On the table in front of Don are .45 caliber, .38 caliber and .22 caliber handguns. Don has arms folded over his chest and is staring blankly at the far wall. He remains motionless for a minute, then reaches into duffel bag for ammunition and begins loading the pistols. After loading, he chambers each one and pushes the safety on, then places all three weapons inside the duffel bag.

Don gets up, picks up the duffel bag and exits the apartment. He locks door and walks to his old car, places the duffel bag in the right front passenger seat, starts engine and drives away.

Don exits his apartment complex and turns east on I-70. Highway sign indicates Jefferson City to be thirty miles ahead.

Don's jaw set and eyes reflect resolute determination as he drives toward Jefferson City.

Gradually, his face and eyes indicate his determination is fading.

Don proceeds for a few more miles, then takes an exit ramp with a McDonald's in sight. He pulls into the lot, gets out and walks to the order counter behind a young woman.

INT. McDONALD'S RESTAURANT – NOON

Don stands silently in line with a troubled expression.

Don buys cheeseburger, fries and coffee and finds an empty table where he sits with food in front of him. He stares blankly ahead for a minute or so, then slowly eats his lunch with perplexed appearance. He finishes lunch, returns to car, starts engine and drives out of McDonald's lot.

EXT. INTERSTATE 70 WESTBOUND LANES – EARLY AFTERNOON

Don heads back to Columbia. He appears to be at ease with himself.

EXT. DON'S APARTMENT COMPLEX – EARLY AFTERNOON

Don's car pulls up to his apartment. He parks, gets out, retrieves the duffel bag, walks to his apartment, unlocks door and disappears inside.

INT. DON'S APARTMENT – EARLY AFTERNOON

Don sits down at table and removes handguns from duffel bag; then unloads each one and returns all three to the bag. The wall phone in kitchen rings. Don gets up and answers.

Don

Hello.........

Don listens for about twenty seconds.

Don

No.....I don't think Mr. Alexander would
be interested in your
publication. He had no further interest in law
and order.......and he doesn't
live here any more........

SLOW FADE TO BLACK SCREEN

www.ingramcontent.com/pod-product-compliance
Lightning Source LLC
Chambersburg PA
CBHW051520170526
45165CB00002B/546